RENOIR

Elizabeth Elias Kaufman

CASTLE
BOOKS

A Division of
BOOK SALES, INC.
110 Enterprise Avenue
Secaucus, NJ. 07094

Copyright © 1980 Ottenheimer Publishers, Inc.
All Rights Reserved. Printed in U.S.A.

ISBN: 0-89009-373-3

CONTENTS

His Times .... Page 5

His Life 7

His Works 8

COLOR ILLUSTRATIONS

Plate 1 Pont Neuf .... Page 17

      2 The Fishing Pole 18

      3 Woman at the Piano 19

      4 Young Woman Braiding Her Hair 20

      5 By the River Bend 21

      6 Bouquet in Front of a Mirror 22

      7 Georges Rivière 23

      8 Portrait of the Actress Jeanne Samary — detail 24

      9 Portrait of a Girl 25

    10 The Umbrellas — detail 26

    11 Study for The Umbrellas, The Modiste ... 27

    12 Nude 28

    13 Marine 29

    14 Moslem Feast in Algiers 30

    15 Portrait of Théodore de Banville 31

    16 The Harvester 32

    17 Mosque at Algiers 33

    18 Girl in a Straw Hat 34

    19 Two Little Girls Reading 35

    20 The English Peartree 36

    21 Seated Nude 37

Plate 22	Boating	Page 38
23	Countess de Portales	39
24	Child with Brown Hair	40
25	Fishermen's Houses at Les Martigues	41
26	Two Girls Reading	42
27	Bather Drying Her Foot	43
28	Gabrielle with Jean	44
29	Mother and Child	45
30	Woman Reading	46
31	Anemones	47
32	Portrait of a Child	48
33	Landscape	49
34	Jean Renoir Sewing	50
35	Coco	51
36	La Toilette	52
37	Coco Painting	53
38	Lady with a Fan	54
39	Gabrielle and Her Jewels	55
40	Landscape, Cagnes	56
41	Self-Portrait	57
42	Mme Durand-Ruel	58
43	Seated Nude	59
44	Demi-nude	60
45	Woman with a Hat	61
46	Woman in a Flowered Hat	62
47	Child with a Teddy Bear	63
48	The Bathers	64

RENOIR

Renoir, master of sunlight and happiness, is most famous as a creator of beautiful women and children. He was a man who believed in hard work. When his fortunes changed and he was no longer struggling for fame and money, he continued working as hard as before. For the last twenty years of his life, he suffered from arthritis. It became so severe that he was confined to a wheelchair and could only paint with a brush strapped to his arm. But the arthritis did not stop him, for Renoir was a man who loved to create.

Although he was influenced by many other artists, in the end, he achieved a style that was uniquely his own. To understand his art, it is best to begin with the state of art during the early nineteenth century.

HIS TIMES

The nineteenth century was a transitional period in art history. In order to understand its importance, one must recognize that there is a close relationship between art, the overall cultural climate, and the world in general. The most striking example of this relationship is, of course, the Renaissance. The Middle Ages produced little that was new. Creative thinking, if not forbidden, was certainly not encouraged. The Renaissance led to a renewed interest in philosophy, learning, and cultural creativity. Artists of the Renaissance searched for new ways to express their ideas. In this same manner, the art of the nineteenth century presents an accurate reflection of the changing world in which it was produced.

As the pace of life quickened, the number and nature of art styles changed. While the eighteenth century was largely confined to the Baroque, the Rococo, and Neoclassical styles; the nineteenth century gave birth to Romanticism, Realism, Impressionism, Post-Impressionism, and Expressionism. It also laid the groundwork for styles such as Fauvism and Cubism.

The most important aspect of these new styles is the concept that underlies them. Each movement was created by artists seeking new ways to express themselves. There was a determined effort to free art from tradition. This often resulted in sharp clashes between artists and art critics as nineteenth century artists struggled to free themselves and their art from the conservatism that characterized the ruling art bodies.

As each of these new movements became accepted, artists tried to break away from them. Thus, a "new" movement was never new for long. Once it was established, rules and boundaries were drawn around it. This provoked a reaction. Art became a very intellectual and rebellious exercise.

Romanticism was the dominant art movement at the beginning of the nineteenth century. The Romantics were interested in portraying romance, nature, and adventure. The works they created were highly emotional and utilized color to a much greater degree than previous styles.

When Romanticism had become the accepted style, a new movement started. The Realists, unlike the Romantics, based their art on their personal experiences. These artists did not paint anything they had not seen or experienced. They did not paint seascapes unless they had been there. Historical scenes, angels, and the like disappeared from their work. Gustave Courbet was the acknowledged leader of Realism. He and his followers caused a tremendous stir. The art public and the critics considered their work undignified. Having accepted Romanticism, they were unprepared for scenes of men working on roads.

By 1863, when Edouard Manet painted **Le Dejeuner sur l'Herbe (Luncheon on the Grass),** Realism was the accepted style. Manet's piece is usually thought of as the first Impressionistic painting. Although it was an early work, it contains many of the characteristics that were later associated with Impressionism. If the Realists had caused a stir, Manet and the early Impressionists created an explosion in the art world.

The title of "Impressionism" was bestowed upon the new style by a disdainful art critic. It was taken from the title of a painting by Claude Monet, **Impression: Sunrise.** The name of the new style was considered quite derogatory. At the time, art was supposed to have a higher purpose. It was expected to be more than an artist's impression. In defiance of tradition the Impressionists refused to make religious, moral, or political statements. In fact, many of them preferred to paint flowers and landscapes.

Because the visual reality was all important to the Impressionists, they concentrated on color and light. The use of line was almost abandoned. Color, not line, was used to model and shape. Shadows were created by deepening the original color instead of using the more traditional browns and blacks. The emphasis on color and light, the elimination of many details, and the infrequent use of line resulted in somewhat flat images.

The importance of visual reality was at least partially responsible for the most obvious characteristic of Impressionism, the short brushstroke. This was used in an attempt to finish the painting quickly before the light shifted, changing the visual reality. Perhaps more importantly, the short brushstroke produced a shimmering, dappled quality similar to the natural effect of light striking an object.

During the nineteenth century, the French art world was controlled by the Ecole des Beaux Arts (the Academy of Fine Arts). Through its official exhibition of new works, the Salon, the Academy dictated public tastes. Only officially approved styles were accepted for exhibition at the Salon. At the time, there was no such thing as a one-man show at art galleries. Because they had no other way to establish their reputation or to exhibit their works to the public, artists whose works were rejected by the Academy for the Salon could expect only limited success.

However, by 1863, so many works were being rejected and there was so much anger and discontent among the rejected artists, that the government realized it had to do something. In May of 1863, the government sponsored a separate exhibition called the Salon des Refusés. Held in the Palais de l'Industrie, the exhibition was open to any artist whose works had been rejected by the Academy's Salon. Many of the early Impressionists exhibited in this way.

In order to understand the influence of his times on Renoir, it is important to remember that his development as an artist occurred during a period when art was in a state of flux. In his early work, he was influenced by eighteenth century painters such as Watteau and Fragonard. The Realist Courbet was a powerful force in his art for a time, as were the Old Masters. His contemporaries were much more radical than he. Most were strongly opposed to traditional art. A portion of these friends, the Impressionists, eventually exerted a tremendous influence on Renoir. However, he never surrendered his interest in Classical art. In his best works, it is the synthesis of many styles that characterizes Renoir's greatness.

HIS LIFE

Pierre-Auguste Renoir was born on February 25, 1841 in the French city of Limoges. His father, Léonard, was a tailor. His mother, Marguerite, had been a seamstress. Until he was four years old, the family lived with Léonard's father. When his grandfather died in 1845, the family moved to Paris.

Renoir's scholastic education ended in 1854, when he was thirteen. There were at least two reasons for this. First of all, his family was not wealthy, and he knew he would need to learn a trade. However, of greater importance, Renoir was not a scholar. He seems to have spent a great deal of time in school drawing in his notebooks. This habit can be traced to the many visits he made to the Louvre and to his natural talents as an artist.

In 1854, Renoir had to make a choice of careers. He had an excellent voice and was encouraged to follow a musical career. However, his father disapproved. Instead, Renoir pursued his other skill and was apprenticed to a ceramics factory as a porcelain decorator. As a former resident of Limoges, his father approved of this choice.

For four years, from 1854 until 1858, Renoir worked for the Lévy Frères ceramic works. Although he started at the bottom creating small bouquets of flowers, he advanced quickly. By 1858, he had progressed to painting the profile of Marie Antoinette and finally to figure painting.

Unfortunately, the factory made plans to mechanize a large percentage of the work. This meant that Renoir had to find a new occupation. He became a fan painter. This job did not provide enough money, so he supplemented his income by decorating walls in Parisian cafés. Next, he accepted a job painting blinds for the windows of missionaries to Africa. While working in these jobs, he was also spending time in the Louvre. It is clear that around 1861 he decided to become a painter. Although the jobs mentioned above did not earn him a great deal of money, the time he spent in them was not wasted. His work had exposed him to the great eighteenth century painters. His visits to the Louvre had taught him about the Old Masters, and his friends had exposed him to the radical trends in modern art.

Renoir enrolled in the Academy of Fine Arts, studying with Gleyre. There he seems to have been one of the few students to take the work seriously. This was in keeping with his background as a craftsman. It was a discipline he maintained throughout his career. By 1862, Renoir had a circle of friends that included Sisley, Monet, and Bazille. Monet was the leader of the group. It was he who prodded the others to join him in painting sessions in the forest of Fontainbleau.

Painting outside was not new. However, older artists had done sketches, studies, or watercolors outside and then returned to their studios to complete the work. That the entire piece should be painted at the scene became a basic tenet of Impressionism, tied to the concept of visual reality.

During the next few years, Renoir continued to mature as an artist. In addition to Sisley, Bazille, and Monet, he was influenced by the work of Courbet, Manet, and Diaz. His art during this period changed with almost every piece as he tried to reconcile different styles and ideas. His changing art resulted in mixed reactions from the official art world. His entries in the Salon of the Academy of Fine Arts were rejected in 1866 and 1867, but accepted in 1868.

The Franco-Prussian War interrupted the artist's career in 1870. Along with several of his friends, Renoir served in a cavalry regiment. Although he returned to Paris in 1871, his good friend Bazille was not so fortunate. He had been killed in the fighting.

Renoir met the art dealer Durand-Ruel through Monet. At first, the dealer was not very impressed with Renoir's work. He bought **Pont Neuf** (plate 1) from Renoir, but in the beginning that was his only purchase. However, within ten years, he became one of Renoir's most ardent supporters.

The group of artists with whom Renoir worked decided to hold their own exhibition in 1873. This was the first group exhibition of Impressionism. It was organized as a protest to the official exhibition of the Salon. Because of the adverse reaction to the show, the group held an auction instead of an exhibition the next year. In 1876 and 1877, the group exhibitions were resumed. Although he had participated in the auction and in the other exhibitions, Renoir did not enter the one in 1879. Instead, he submitted an entry to the Salon and was accepted.

During 1881, Renoir traveled quite a bit. He was in the process of changing styles and trying to find himself as an artist. In the spring he went to Algiers where he painted **Moslem Feast in Algiers** (plate 14). Later in the year he visited Italy.

In 1882, he married Aline Charigot whom he had met several years earlier. Their first child, Pierre, was born in 1885. A second son, Jean, was born in 1894, and a third son, Claude, nicknamed "Coco", was born in 1901. Renoir always enjoyed painting his children. They are seen in intimate moments such as **Boating** (plate 22), **Gabrielle with Jean** (plate 28), and **Coco Painting** (plate 37).

The end of Renoir's life was filled with pain. In 1894 he suffered the first of numerous bouts of arthritis. By 1910 he was confined to a wheelchair. Finally, he could only paint if someone strapped the brush to his hand. The pain was not only physical. Between 1914 and 1915, his wife died and his two eldest sons, Pierre and Jean, were severely wounded in World War I.

None of the pain stopped him from working. The sunny disposition, the belief in hard work, and his love of creating persisted until his death on December 3, 1919.

HIS WORKS

PLATE 1

Renoir painted several scenes of Paris streets. This one, **Pont Neuf,** was created in 1872. It is a fairly complicated work showing the bridge, people and carriages, the buildings on the other side of the bridge, and quite a bit of sky. The artist included many details. Notice, for example, the detail work on the lamp posts and on the women's costumes. It is evident that the piece was painted with the sun in Renoir's eyes, not an easy task in itself, and one which makes it more difficult to include details.

The colors and shapes are beautifully contrasted. While the tones are essentially cool (dominated by blues), both the people and the buildings have yellow, red, and white accents. The shapes of the clouds balance the lines of the buildings. Many of the elements of Impressionism are present, but it is obvious that Renoir was using techniques from other styles as well. This is typical of the work he produced at the time in that it is not totally Impressionistic.

One of the basic tenets of Impressionism is that the work should be completed on the scene. Renoir was aided in painting **Pont Neuf** by his brother who would stop pedestrians, ask them lengthy questions, and thus delay them. This allowed Renoir to quickly sketch them in place.

PLATE 2

The Fishing Pole was created in about 1875. The drawing of the woman is fairly complete. Behind her is the beginning of a sketch of a reclining male figure. Although incomplete, the male figure is very reminiscent of Manet's work in *Le Dejeuner sur l'Herbe (Luncheon on the Grass)* painted in 1863.

PLATE 3

During the beginning of his career, Renoir was unsure of his style. He was influenced by a number of different artists. Consequently, his early work was created in a variety of styles. Frequently, more than one influence can be detected in a single work. Such is the case with *Woman at the Piano.* Much of the technique in this piece belongs to the Impressionists, including both the elimination of many details and the brushstroke work. A hint of Manet's style can be seen in the dark bands which accent the woman's dress. The coloring shows the subtle influence of Delacroix.

PLATE 4

The wistful gaze of the *Young Woman Braiding Her Hair* has a beautiful dreamlike quality. The artist has given the viewer an opportunity to observe a very private moment in the girl's life. The entire work has a delicacy that is characteristic of Renoir's style.

PLATE 5

Painted in 1876, *By the River Bend* is totally unlike the other work Renoir created that year. In contrast with *Young Woman Braiding Her Hair* (plate 4) and *Bouquet in Front of a Mirror* (plate 6), the colors are earthy and muted. The mood of the painting is somber and somewhat gloomy.

Renoir is best known as a painter of happy scenes. *By the River Bend* is an exception to his usual sunny pictures. The style is a mixture of Impressionistic techniques and Realistic subject matter.

PLATE 6

The *Bouquet in Front of a Mirror,* painted in about 1876, is almost a *tour de force.* The Impressionistic style is especially well suited here. The flowers are executed with the short brushstrokes the Impressionists favored. The image in the mirror is even more Impressionistic. Notice the extra touches Renoir has added. The vase is decorated with flowers to compliment the bouquet. On the table rests one dying petal. The Impressionistic technique involved painting from life. Renoir, no doubt, began the work with fresh flowers. As the work progressed, the blossoms began to wilt. It is probable, therefore, that Renoir added the fallen petal when the work was almost complete.

PLATE 7

In 1877, Renoir painted a portrait of his good friend *Georges Rivière.* The work is highly Impressionistic. One of the devices the artist used to create this effect was to paint the piece on a rough tile. The irregular surface with its uneven texture gives the portrait an added dimension. This is one of the few paintings Renoir created on tile.

PLATE 8

This detail from the *Portrait of the Actress Jeanne Samary* shows the woman's beautiful face. Renoir painted several portraits of Jeanne Samary. This one was created in 1878. In 1879, the artist entered one of her portraits in the Salon. Because he entered the Salon, he did not take part in the group Impressionism exhibition that year.

PLATE 9

As was the case with many of his female portraits during the late 1870's, the **Portrait of a Girl** uses a languid head-on-hand pose. This piece, created in 1878, is strongly Impressionistic. The distant gaze, the blurring of unimportant details, and the color work give the piece a soft, dreamlike quality. The viewer can't help but wonder what the girl was thinking about during the moment Renoir captured in the painting.

Within two years of painting **Portrait of a Girl,** Renoir's style changed. Although elements of Impressionism remained in his work throughout his career, the viewer can see the change occurring by comparing this work with **Nude** (plate 12) painted in 1880 and with **Girl in a Straw Hat** (plate 18) painted in 1885.

PLATE 10

The Umbrellas was painted between 1879 and 1882. It is an interesting work in many ways. The painting fascinates art scholars because it is a transitional piece. During the 1870's, Renoir's work was essentially Impressionistic. Towards the end of the decade, he became disenchanted with that style. Renoir felt Impressionism was overly dependent on light and did not give enough attention to line and form.

The detail illustrated here is from the right-hand side of the painting. The child's face and the details of her costume are Impressionistic, as are the other figures on the right-hand side. They were executed in about 1879. The rest of the work was painted later in Renoir's new style. Thus, **The Umbrellas** exhibits two distinct artistic styles.

PLATE 11

This **Study for the Umbrellas, The Modiste** is an indication of Renoir's new interest in line and form. The typical Impressionistic approach to painting involved a bare minimum of sketch work. The artist found what he wanted to paint, he studied it with his eyes, and then he painted it. By the early 1880's, Renoir felt that Impressionism did not give enough emphasis to composition. Thus, he began to do a larger number of sketches to help develop the line, form, and composition he wanted in his work.

The figure in this sketch does not appear in exactly the same pose in **The Umbrellas** (plate 10). However, the main figure on the left-hand side of the painting bears a strong resemblance to the woman in the sketch.

PLATE 12

It was not until the 1880's that Renoir began to paint nudes. The Impressionists did not usually portray nudes. However, Renoir's new emphasis on line and form, and his reawakened interest in Classical subjects and techniques led him to produce quite a large number of nudes during the rest of his career.

This **Nude** was painted in 1880. Notice the difference between the woman's face here and the faces in **Portrait of the Actress Jeanne Samary** (plate 8) and **Portrait of a Girl** (plate 9). This face shows Renoir's growing interest in the use of line.

PLATE 13

Renoir spent the summer of 1880 at Croissy. It is believed that **Marine** was executed there. This watercolor is one of the last totally Impressionistic works Renoir created. Even the seascape subject matter is typically Impressionistic. It is not known whether Renoir expected to use **Marine** as the basis for an oil painting, or whether he considered this to be a finished work. In any event, the blending of the colors and the tones themselves make this watercolor a beautiful piece.

PLATE 14

Early in 1881, Renoir left Paris to visit Algiers. The journey was made in an effort to see what had so inspired Delacroix. Although it was the rainy season, Renoir was deeply impressed by the character of the sun and light he found in Algiers.

Moslem Feast in Algiers, painted during this visit, displays his attempt to capture the mood and feel of the scene. To convey the effects of sunlight, the artist used a large amount of white, accented with shades of blue and purple. Most of the figures are only a blur, executed with a few strokes of his brush.

Renoir did not stay in Algiers for long. He grew bored with the city. He enjoyed painting women, but the women of Algiers did not appeal to him in the way Parisian women did. Almost a year after *Moslem Feast in Algiers* was painted, Renoir returned to the city to recuperate from an illness. During his second visit he painted *Mosque at Algiers* (plate 17) a very similar work.

PLATE 15

Portrait of Théodore de Banville was created 1881 using pastels. The man was a friend of Renoir's and was often present at intellectual gatherings in Paris. One can see quite a bit of the man's personality in this work. His sensitive eyes are accentuated by his raised eyebrows. Renoir shows the viewer the man's age in two subtle ways. Just above the ears there is a hint of white hair pushing out from under the hat. Below the chin, the subject's neck is very wrinkled. The grain of the paper, visible in the face, but more pronounced in the jacket, provides an added effect. Although more famous for his portraits of women, Renoir also painted quite a few male portraits early in his career.

PLATE 16

Renoir shows his new interest in line and form in *The Harvester,* sketched in about 1882. Although incomplete, the figure of the woman has great bulk. This was in keeping with his feelings about Classicism. Renoir's interest in solidifying the forms and figures in his work is characteristic of Post-Impressionism. He never lost his interest in the effects of light and color, but he began to use those effects to enhance his work rather than allowing them to dominate as they had in his Impressionistic phase.

PLATE 17

In 1882, Renoir visited his friend and fellow artist, Cézanne. During his visit, he became ill and finally had to leave. He went to Algiers to recuperate. *Mosque at Algiers,* like *Moslem Feast in Algiers* (plate 14) painted a year earlier, shows the effect of intense sunlight on Renoir's work. The entire painting is suffused with a steady, even light.

The trips Renoir made during the early 1880's are an indication of the restlessness he felt about his work. Although he knew he wanted to make changes, he was very unsure about their direction. He even began to question his abilities as an artist. What is interesting about the paintings he created in Algiers is that they show little if any of the changes he was making.

PLATE 18

During the 1880's, Renoir developed a new style. It is usually referred to as his "harsh period" or *manière aigre,* his "sour manner". *Girl in a Straw Hat* is a perfect example of this style. The subject is clearly defined in both line and form. Her face and body have a definite mass. The details are quite clear. The change in style is obvious when *Girl in a Straw Hat* is compared with *Young Woman Braiding Her Hair* (plate 4) or with *Portrait of a Girl* (plate 9). Both of these earlier works are highly Impressionistic.

PLATE 19

Two Little Girls Reading, created in about 1885, is one of a large number of works Renoir produced using children as the subject matter. Often, as here, the children are little girls. Few other artists have been able to portray children so realistically and so beautifully. This pastel sketch is obviously not complete. Nevertheless, the poses are so natural the viewer does not notice the missing details.

During the 1880's, as Renoir broke away from Impressionism, he made many sketches in order to sharpen his skills. In *Two Little Girls Reading,* he was working on composition and on solidifying forms.

PLATE 20

By 1885, when *The English Peartree* was painted, Renoir was well into his "harsh period". He felt that Impressionism did not give enough emphasis to line, form, and composition. Most of his art during this period is indeed "harsher" than the work created in his Impressionistic style. However, his landscape work continued to be Impressionistic. In this piece, the artist has placed more emphasis on composition than before. Notice also the increased use of shadows.

PLATE 21

Beginning in the 1880's, Renoir sketched and painted nudes. This *Seated Nude* was produced during the late 1880's. The harsh style with its heavy dependence on line can be compared with *La Toilette* (plate 36) painted in 1902 in his mature style.

Seated Nude is a good example of Renoir's attempt to reconcile several different styles. The Classical influence is obvious here. Through the use of line, Renoir created a figure with tremendous bulk. There is no hint of Impressionism in *Seated Nude.*

PLATE 22

Renoir's first son was born in 1885. *Boating,* created in 1886, shows the artist's wife holding their infant son, Pierre. The piece exhibits an impressive stability. The bare outline of the boat balances the strong pyramid of the mother and her child. The background consists of a few fanciful flowers behind the woman's head.

This is a very Classical pose, reminiscent of the works of the Old Masters. However, Renoir makes the piece his own by giving his wife a serene, yet highly individualized expression. This is no idealized Madonna, just as Pierre is not an idealized Christ Child.

PLATE 23

By 1888, when the *Countess de Portàles* was painted, Renoir was moving from his harsh period into his mature style. He has incorporated elements of both Impressionism and his harsh style into this work. Instead of an over reliance on light and color, Renoir used these effects to develop the form and figure. Instead of relying on line, he used line along with color to build volume. The woman is portrayed in a soft delicate manner that is characteristic of Renoir's work.

PLATE 24

The *Child with Brown Hair* was painted between 1887 and 1888. Although the name of the subject is not known, Renoir's feelings of warmth and tenderness towards children is very obvious here. The piece is transitional. It falls between his harsh period and his mature style. The total dependence on line is gone, but the iridescent softness that is characteristic of his later works is only partially present. The difference can be seen when *Child with Brown Hair* is compared with *Two Girls Reading* (plate 26). The second work was created between 1890 and 1891.

PLATE 25

After visiting Cézanne, Renoir spent part of the winter of 1888 at Martigues, where he created the beautiful watercolor, *Fishermen's Houses at Les Martigues.* The piece is perfectly balanced by color and composition. Notice how each color is reflected in several parts of the work. For example, the purplish color in the right-hand corner of the sky is also seen in the lake and in the foreground.

PLATE 26

Renoir is famous for his ability to depict young girls. He painted a number of works that illustrate young girls involved in different activities. *Two Girls Reading,* painted between 1890 and 1891, is one of the most beautiful of this genre. As was frequently the case, the subjects are dressed in summer clothes and wear large, soft hats.

Renoir's style as seen in *Two Girls Reading* is referred to as his "iridescent period" or his "pearly style". The soft, glowing skin tones found in this piece were only gradually replaced by a slightly ruddier color.

PLATE 27

In addition to his fame as a painter of children, Renoir is known as a superb creator of female nudes. Although he was criticized for painting them so frequently, Renoir's nudes represent some of his finest works. This *Bather Drying Her Foot,* created in 1890 is a typical pose. The woman is completely absorbed in her task. The artist is not trying to make a statement here, he is merely reporting an intimate event.

Renoir used white chalk to give this sketch a shiny, wet feel. The black strokes add volume and form to the woman's figure.

PLATE 28

After the birth of their second son, the Renoirs hired Gabrielle Renard as a nurse. This young woman was related to Renoir's wife. Although she did serve as a nurse for Jean, Renoir frequently used her as a model. In fact, she lived with the family for approximately twenty years.

Gabrielle with Jean was created in 1895, when Jean was a year old. The work, done in pastels, focuses attention on the infant. This effect was achieved through the use of ruddy reds and earthy colors as a contrast to the white of Jean's costume.

PLATE 29

Mother and Child, painted in about 1895, is extraordinarily well balanced. The figures are developed to form a triangle. The woman's head forms the top, her back one of the sides, her face along with the child's face and the cat form the other side.

The painting is not only balanced geometrically, it is also balanced by color. The tones of the woman's hair are reflected in the cat's fur and in the bands across the bottom of her skirt. The cool tones of her skirt are balanced by the warmer tones of the background to the left.

The scene catches the participants in a moment of humorous domestic action. The child is more interested in the cat than in changing clothes.

PLATE 30

In *Woman Reading,* the artist balances the subdued tones of the background with the vibrant color of the woman's dress. The splashes of white in her dress, hat, and the letter she holds are held in check by the black accents in her hat and the bands of black around her waist.

Painted in about 1895, the piece is one of Renoir's most charming works. The beautiful woman, seen in profile, is totally absorbed in reading her letter. Her fanciful hat, tilted because of the angle of her head, provides a counterweight to the angle of her back.

PLATE 31

Renoir loved to paint beauty. It was natural that he should enjoy painting flowers. Unlike his good friend Monet, he did not devote himself to painting them, and they are usually seen as still life works rather than in their natural state. However, Renoir's composition in **Anemones** is such that the flowers almost seem to be in the ground rather than in a vase. The top flowers appear alive and fresh, the ones on the sides seem to be stretching for the sun. Near the handle of the vase, one blossom droops, past its prime.

PLATE 32

The model for **Portrait of a Child** is not known. The work was created in about 1900. Renoir's second son, Jean, would have been six years old, probably too old to have been the model here. His third son, Claude (nicknamed "Coco"), was not born until 1901.

The bow in the hair is misleading for modern viewers who think of bows as being feminine. Renoir's children, all sons, are frequently depicted in his work with bows.

PLATE 33

In December of 1898, Renoir experienced a severe attack of arthritis. For the remainder of his life, the artist was plagued by the disease. By 1912, he was forced to use a wheelchair. However, the arthritis did not stop him from working. **Landscape,** created in about 1900, is a good example of his continuing ability and his desire to work despite the pain he endured. The piece was executed in watercolors. The tones seem to flow and blend with perfect harmony. Each color complements another and is echoed in several different parts of the work.

PLATE 34

Jean Renoir Sewing was painted in about 1900. It shows Renoir's second son concentrating on his task. In this piece, Renoir reveals his skill in using the effects of light. Although his Impressionistic phase had ended approximately twenty years earlier, Renoir always maintained an interest in light and color. Here, the light bounces off of every surface, giving the painting a glowing radiance.

To balance the predominate warm colors, Renoir used a cool blue background. Notice that the skin tones in the hands closely resemble the colors in the shirt.

PLATE 35

The third of Renoir's three sons, Claude, was born in 1901. Nicknamed **Coco,** the child appears in many of Renoir's works. This portrait was painted in about 1902. In contrast with **Jean Renoir Sewing** (plate 34), executed approximately two years earlier, the color contrast is not as strong. Additionally, Coco's face is not as clearly defined as is Jean's. The reason for this difference is not known.

PLATE 36

La Toilette was painted in 1902. The subject was one that the artist used many times during his mature years. The woman's figure is realistic but executed in such a way as to soften the edges and the curves. The beautiful nude is enhanced by the somewhat Impressionistic background.

The work is interesting because of the dynamic contrast between the face and body. The voluptuous figure is paired with a young, naive face.

PLATE 37

In 1906, Renoir's youngest son was five years old. *Coco Painting* shows the boy at a small easel. During the first decade of the twentieth century, Coco was one of Renoir's favorite models. The artist drew him in many different poses, holding objects, involved in various activities, and just sitting at a table. Notice that Coco's face here, as in *Coco* (plate 35), is not clearly defined.

PLATE 38

The serene *Lady with a Fan* is one of Renoir's loveliest portraits. The detail work is subordinated to the beautiful face. Renoir repeats the flowers in her hair with a flower-like border in her dress.

At one time early in his career, Renoir earned a living painting fans. Here, the fan is unadorned and serves only to add to the feeling of quiet wealth. Notice that the lines of the fan are echoed in the upper left-hand corner of the work. These lines help to balance the sensuous curves of the woman's body.

PLATE 39

For approximately twenty years, Gabrielle Renard was one of Renoir's favorite models. Originally hired as a nurse for the artist's son, Jean, she often spent more time posing for Renoir than supervising the child. She remained with the family even after the Renoir children were grown.

Renoir was fascinated by the color and tone of Gabrielle's skin and by the way it reflected light. In fact, people joked at the time that all one needed to be employed by the Renoir family was to have beautiful skin.

Gabrielle and Her Jewels was created in about 1910. Like most of his work at the time, it contains quite a bit of red. In this case, the red is balanced by the white accents of her robe and by her dark hair.

PLATE 40

In contrast with *Landscape* (plate 33), created in about 1900, *Landscape, Cagnes* from 1910 is much more dependent upon line. The piece gives the viewer an opportunity to examine Renoir's approach to his art. It is obvious that the artist began by sketching in pen. He appears to have been primarily concerned with the general outline of the buildings and trees. Evidently the work was never finished, because in the lower right-hand corner Renoir sketched what might be a small bridge. The detail work around it is missing.

PLATE 41

Although not known as a painter of self-portraits, Renoir actually created quite a few of them. This *Self-Portrait* was painted in 1910, when the artist was sixty-nine years old. Despite his obvious age, the piece is not gloomy. Renoir shows himself as a fairly rugged individual. There is a basic simplicity and sweetness inherent in the work. Renoir was a man who believed in hard work and who considered himself to be a lucky man. Those feelings come through very clearly in this piece.

PLATE 42

In 1901, Renoir had painted a portrait of the art dealer, Paul Durand-Ruel. This man had been extremely helpful to the artist by promoting his works. In 1911, Renoir painted the portrait of *Mme Durand-Ruel.*

The colors have been carefully chosen. The purple of her dress is contrasted with the yellow-gold of her shawl. In the upper left-hand corner, Renoir has placed a vase of yellow and red flowers. The flower motif is continued in the wallpaper in the upper right-hand corner, but there the flowers are purple with yellow centers. This is a much busier, complex work than his *Lady with a Fan* (plate 38) created four years earlier.

PLATE 43

Renoir's love of the female form is obvious in the work he produced during the last ten years of his life. During this period, he painted and drew nudes in many poses, but most frequently as bathers. *Seated Nude*, produced in 1916, is an excellent example of his mature style. The woman's figure is monumental, occupying approximately three-fourths of the entire work. The skin seems almost translucent. There is a languid, fluid quality to the body that is typical of Renoir's female figures.

PLATE 44

Demi-nude was probably created between 1916 and 1918. The presence of so much black makes it slightly unusual, especially when compared with some of the other nudes Renoir produced at the same time. It is also different in that the background is rather stark. These differences become clear when *Demi-Nude* is compared with *Seated Nude* (plate 43) and with *The Bathers* (plate 48).

PLATES 45, 46

Woman with a Hat (plate 45) and *Woman in a Flowered Hat* (plate 46) were created between 1916 and 1918. These two pastel works display Renoir's fondness for female hats. Sometimes they are elegant as in *Woman with a Hat,* and sometimes fanciful as seen in *Woman in a Flowered Hat.*

Woman with a Hat is more typical of Renoir's work in that the woman gazes out rather than down. However, both works show the same delicate modeling of the face.

Woman in a Flowered Hat is the more complex of the two. Her hat is a symphony of colors and dominates the work. In the lower left-hand corner of this piece, Renoir worked on several other faces.

PLATE 47

Although much of the detail work is missing, *Child with a Teddy Bear* is one of Renoir's most appealing paintings. The charm of the piece is due to the relationship the artist developed between the child and her toy. This was achieved in part by giving both the same plaintive expression. To reinforce the effect, Renoir used colors to enhance the mood.

The work is thought to have been created between 1916 and 1918. By that time, Renoir was crippled with arthritis. He was confined to a wheelchair and could only paint with a brush strapped to his hand. Yet, art scholars feel that his work was not hindered by his disability. The effect created in *Child with a Teddy Bear* was the result of deliberate planning, not of his illness.

PLATE 48

The Bathers is very typical of the work Renoir produced during the last ten years of his life. In that period he painted a profusion of nudes. They are beautiful expressions of the female form. In this piece, created between 1916 and 1918, the nudes are placed against an abstract landscape that serves as a background. Because of the use of color and the skillfully controlled composition, the nudes seem to blend into their surroundings.

Plate 1 Pont Neuf, 1872, oil on canvas, 2′ 5⅝″ × 3′ ⅞″, National Gallery of Art, Washington, D. C.

Plate 2 The Fishing Pole, c. 1875, sanguine and pastel with white, whereabouts unknown

Plate 3 Woman at the Piano, c. 1875, oil on canvas,
3′ ¾″ × 2′ 5¼″, Art Institute, Chicago

Plate 4 Young Woman Braiding Her Hair, 1876, oil on canvas, 21⅞" × 18¼", National Gallery of Art, Washington, D. C.

Plate 5 By the River Bend, 1876, oil on canvas, 22¾" × 27⅝", private collection

Plate 6 Bouquet in Front of a Mirror, c. 1876, oil on canvas, 3′ ⅝″ × 2′ 4⅜″, private collection

Plate 7 Georges Rivière, 1877, oil on tile, 14½″ × 11½″, National Gallery of Art, Washington, D. C.

Plate 8 Portrait of the Actress Jeanne Samary, detail — her face, 1878, oil on canvas, Hermitage, Leningrad

Plate 9 Portrait of a Girl, 1878, oil on canvas, 25½″ × 21¼″, private collection

Plate 10 The Umbrellas, detail — child's head, c. 1879-82, oil on canvas, National Gallery, London

Plate 11 Study for The Umbrellas, The Modiste, c. 1882, sanguine heightened with white, private collection

Plate 12 Nude, 1880, oil on canvas, 2′ 8″ × 2′ 1½″, Musée Rodin, Paris

Plate 13 Marine, 1880, watercolor, whereabouts unknown

Plate 14 Moslem Feast in Algiers, 1881, oil on canvas, 2′ 4¾″ × 3′ ¼″, Louvre, Paris

Plate 15 Portrait of Théodore de Banville, 1881, pastel,
20½″ × 16¼″, Louvre, Paris

Plate 16 The Harvester, c. 1882, sanguine on paper, whereabouts unknown

Plate 17 Mosque at Algiers, 1882, oil on canvas, 19¼″ × 23¼″, private collection

Plate 18 Girl in a Straw Hat, c. 1884, oil on canvas, 22½" × 18", private collection

Plate 19 Two Little Girls Reading, c. 1885, pastel, 11⅞" × 14 ¾", private collection

Plate 20 The English Peartree, 1885, oil on canvas, private collection

Plate 21 Seated Nude, c. 1885-90, sanguine heightened with white, 14½″ × 11″, private collection

Plate 22 Boating, 1886, watercolor, pen, and lead pencil, 19¾″ × 9⅛″, private collection

Plate 23 Countess de Portàles, 1887, oil on canvas, 3′ 1½″ × 2′ 4¼″, São Paulo Museum, São Paulo

Plate 24 Child with Brown Hair, 1887-88, oil on canvas, 4⅝" × 4",
National Gallery of Art, Washington, D. C.

Plate 25 Fishermen's Houses at Les Martigues, 1888, watercolor,
5⅛″ × 9¼″, Louvre, Paris

Plate 26 Two Girls Reading, 1890-91, oil on canvas, 21¼″ × 19″, Los Angeles County Museum, Los Angeles

Plate 27 Bather Drying Her Foot, 1890, sanguine, black, and white chalk, 22⅞" × 17¾", private collection

Plate 28 Gabrielle with Jean, 1895, pastel, 23½" × 18⅜", private collection

Plate 29 Mother and Child, c. 1895, oil on canvas, 3′ 10″ × 3′ 9″, California Palace of the Legion of Honor, San Francisco

Plate 30 Woman Reading, c. 1895, oil on canvas, 12½″ × 11″, private collection

Plate 31 Anemones, 1898, oil on canvas, 23″ × 19½″, private collection

Plate 32 Portrait of a Child, c. 1900, pastel, whereabouts unknown

Plate 33 Landscape, c. 1900, watercolor, whereabouts unknown

Plate 34 Jean Renoir Sewing, c. 1900, oil on canvas, 21¾″ × 18¼″, Art Institute, Chicago

Plate 35 Coco, c. 1902, oil on canvas, whereabouts unknown

Plate 36 La Toilette, 1902, oil on canvas, 3′ ¼″ × 2′ 4¾″,
Kunsthistorisches, Vienna

Plate 37 Coco Painting, 1906, sanguine heightened with white, 23⅝″ × 15¾″, whereabouts unknown

Plate 38 Lady with a Fan, 1906, oil on canvas, 25⅜″ × 21¼″, private collection

Plate 39 Gabrielle and Her Jewels, c. 1910, oil on canvas,
2′ 8″ × 2′ 1¼″, private collection

Plate 40 Landscape, Cagnes, 1910, pen, pastel, and watercolor, whereabouts unknown

Plate 41 Self-Portrait, 1910, oil on canvas, 18″ × 15″, private collection

Plate 42 Mme Durand-Ruel, 1911, oil on canvas, 3′ ¼″ × 2′ 4¾″, private collection

Plate 43 Seated Nude, 1916, oil on canvas, 2′ 8⅛″ × 2′ 2⅝″, Art Institute, Chicago

Plate 44 Demi-nude, undated, pastel, whereabouts unknown

Plate 45 Woman with a Hat, undated, pastel, whereabouts unknown

Plate 46 Woman in a Flowered Hat, undated, pastel, whereabouts unknown

Plate 47 Child with a Teddy Bear, undated, oil on canvas, private collection

Plate 48 The Bathers, undated, pastel, whereabouts unknown